Elements of
Language
**First
Course**

Sentences and Paragraphs

Skills Practice for Chapters 8–9

- **Student Worksheets**
- **Writers' Reference Sheets**
- **Answer Key**

HOLT, RINEHART AND WINSTON

A Harcourt Classroom Education Company

Austin · New York · Orlando · Atlanta · San Francisco · Boston · Dallas · Toronto · London

STAFF CREDITS

EDITORIAL

Director
Mescal Evler

Manager of Editorial Operations
Bill Wahlgren

Executive Editor
Emily G. Shenk

Project Editor
James E. Eckel

Writing and Editing
Stephanie Wenger, Peggy Ferrin

Copyediting
Michael Neibergall, *Copyediting Manager;* Mary Malone, *Senior Copyeditor;* Joel Bourgeois, Elizabeth Dickson, Gabrielle Field, Jane Kominek, Millicent Ondras, Theresa Reding, Kathleen Scheiner, Laurie Schlesinger, *Copyeditors*

Project Administration
Marie Price, *Managing Editor;* Lori De La Garza, *Editorial Operations Coordinator;* Thomas Browne, Heather Cheyne, Diane Hardin, Mark Holland, Marcus Johnson, Jill O'Neal, Joyce Rector, Janet Riley, Kelly Tankersley, *Project Administration;* Gail Coupland, Ruth Hooker, Margaret Sanchez, *Word Processing*

Editorial Permissions
Janet Harrington, *Permissions Editor*

PRODUCTION

Belinda Barbosa Lopez, *Senior Production Coordinator;* Simira Davis, *Supervisor;* Nancy Hargis, *Media Production Supervisor;* Joan Lindsay, *Production Coordinator;* Beth Prevelige, *Prepress Manager*

MANUFACTURING

Michael Roche, *Supervisor of Inventory and Manufacturing*

ART, DESIGN AND PHOTO

Graphic Services
Kristen Darby, *Manager*

Image Acquisitions
Joe London, *Director;* Tim Taylor, *Photo Research Supervisor;* Rick Benavides, *Assistant Photo Researcher;* Elaine Tate, *Supervisor;* Erin Cone, *Art Buyer*

Cover Design
Sunday Patterson

Printed in the United States of America

ISBN 0-03-056316-X

12345 085 04 03 02 01 00

Table of Contents

Table of Contents *(continued)*

Learning About Paragraphs

for CHAPTER 9

(Pupil's Edition
pp. 288–311)

Table of Contents *(continued)*

About This Book

Revising and Proofreading Handouts

The Blackline Masters

These pages are designed as a reference for students. They include lists of useful words, strategies to improve writing, and aids to proofreading. Encourage students to keep copies of these pages in their subject notebooks or to laminate them and refer to them whenever they begin a significant writing assignment.

Exercises

The Worksheets

Worksheets for each exercise provide students with opportunities to practice what is taught in Part 2 of the Pupil's Edition—how to revise and improve sentences through techniques such as combining sentences and varying sentence lengths. Worksheets also provide students with opportunities to practice the basics of good paragraphs, including how to achieve unity and coherence and how to use effective transitions between paragraphs in longer pieces of writing.

Details and Supporting Sentences

KINDS OF DETAILS	SUPPORTING SENTENCES
Sensory Details	
Sight	The bright sun glared off the front windshield of the car.
Hearing	Thunder boomed down the canyon, echoing off the walls.
Touch	My hands felt frozen to the cold, steel handlebars.
Taste	Thirstily, she gulped down the sweet orange juice.
Smell	The sharp, unpleasant odor of asphalt met his nose.
Facts	In 1998, Mark McGwire slammed seventy home runs in one season to break the record of sixty-one held by Roger Maris.
Examples	Fierce windstorms occur worldwide. For example, tornadoes have wind speeds over 200 miles per hour.

Transitional Words and Phrases

TRANSITIONAL WORDS AND PHRASES

▶ **Comparing and Contrasting Ideas**	also although and another	but however in the same way like	likewise similarly too yet
▶ **Showing Cause and Effect**	as a result because	since	therefore
▶ **Showing Time**	about after at before during finally	first, second, and so on immediately later meanwhile next often	soon then until when
▶ **Showing Place**	above across among around before behind below	beneath beside between by down here in	into near next over there under
▶ **Showing Support**	for example for instance	for this reason	in fact

Types of Paragraphs

Narrative used to tell a story or recount an event	Erik peered beneath the rock and saw a small stone. The stone had a metal ring attached to its center. Erik tugged at the ring and felt the stone move. He pulled harder. Suddenly, the rock lifted. Below it was a dark hole. Erik dropped a pebble down the hole and listened. He heard nothing.
Descriptive used to describe a scene or an object	The narrow front door opens right into the living room. At first the room seems gloomy. As your eyes adjust, you can pick out the many bright spots. The hooked rug in front of the door has reds and yellows in it. On the left wall is a small, blackened fireplace with a cheerful fire burning. Beyond that, two windows face the door. Their heavy curtains let in narrow columns of daylight. On the far side of the room, a tiny fern grows in the sun that streams through the third window.
Expository used to provide information, including facts, instructions, and definitions	Lay the square egg-roll skin on a table with one corner pointing toward you. Put a few spoonsful of filling in the center. Then, take the corner of the skin that is closest to you and fold it over the filling. Next, fold the two side corners inward, using both hands. Then, brush a little beaten egg onto the unfolded corner. Finally, roll the filled part up and over the last corner.
Persuasive used to share opinions and convince others to agree or take action	There are several good reasons for building a new light rail in our city. First, such a railway would reduce the air pollution and noise pollution, which have reached alarming levels. Second, the railway would decrease our parking problems and the traffic jams. Third, building and staffing the railway would create new jobs for the city's workers.

Symbols for Revising and Proofreading

Symbol	Example	Meaning of Symbol
≡	Tucker's homestyle Restaurant.	Capitalize a lowercase letter.
/	the City of Raleigh	Lowercase a capital letter.
∧	a cup of milk	Insert a missing word, letter, or punctuation mark.
℘	How's the that apple?	Leave out a word, letter, or punctuation mark.
∩	frist	Change the order of letters or words.
¶	¶"Go ahead," he said.	Begin a new paragraph.
⊙	She wept⊙	Add a period.
∧	I still apologized however.	Add a comma.

Identifying Sentence Fragments

DIRECTIONS Decide whether the following groups of words are sentence fragments or complete sentences.

- If the word group is a fragment, write *F* on the line provided.
- If it is a sentence, write *S*.

_____ **1.** People and bears on the mountain trails in Glacier National Park.

_____ **2.** A large number of grizzly bears in the park.

_____ **3.** Park rangers teach people how to behave in bear country.

_____ **4.** Want you to stay on the trails.

_____ **5.** Should hike in groups of three or more.

_____ **6.** Want to avoid contact with humans.

_____ **7.** Grizzly bears when they see or hear humans.

_____ **8.** Smart hikers make noise as they hike.

_____ **9.** Talking, clapping their hands, wearing noisy bear bells.

_____ **10.** To let bears know that they are there.

_____ **11.** Mother bears with cubs are the most dangerous.

_____ **12.** If you come across a grizzly bear on the trail.

_____ **13.** People say you should not run.

_____ **14.** Backing away slowly and leaving the area.

_____ **15.** When you are camping in bear country.

_____ **16.** Often not possible to climb a tree.

_____ **17.** If people keep their campsites free of food smells.

_____ **18.** Campers can hang their food supplies from a tree branch.

_____ **19.** Cooking food away from the campsite.

_____ **20.** If people use common sense when hiking or camping in bear country.

Identifying Sentence Fragments

DIRECTIONS Decide whether the following groups of words are sentence fragments or complete sentences.

- If the word group is a fragment, write *F* on the line provided.
- If the word group is a sentence, write *S*.

....

_____ **1.** Amelia Earhart a famous American aviator.

_____ **2.** Earhart was born in 1897 in Atchison, Kansas.

_____ **3.** Was taught to fly an airplane by Neta Snook.

_____ **4.** Setting an unofficial female pilots' altitude record.

_____ **5.** Helped form an organization for women pilots called the Ninety-Nines.

_____ **6.** The first woman to travel by air across the Atlantic Ocean.

_____ **7.** Making Earhart famous.

_____ **8.** Earhart married the famous book publisher George Putnam in 1931.

_____ **9.** After a solo flight across the Atlantic in 1932.

_____ **10.** Wanted to be the first woman to fly around the world.

_____ **11.** Frederick Noonan was Earhart's navigator on this flight.

_____ **12.** Their journey on May 20, 1937.

_____ **13.** Earhart and Noonan took off from Oakland, California, flying east.

_____ **14.** Landing in New Guinea on June 30, and leaving on July 1.

_____ **15.** Earhart sent a radio message saying they were low on fuel.

_____ **16.** Earhart and Noonan never heard from again.

_____ **17.** A search mission for the missing pilots.

_____ **18.** Although it is believed they crashed in the ocean.

_____ **19.** Since no wreckage was ever found.

_____ **20.** The disappearance of Earhart's plane a mystery.

Finding and Revising Fragments

DIRECTIONS Decide which of the following groups of words are sentence fragments.

- If the word group is a fragment, write *F*.
- Revise each fragment by (1) adding a subject, (2) adding a verb, or (3) attaching the fragment to a complete sentence. You may need to change the punctuation and capitalization, too.
- If the word group is already a complete sentence, write *S*.

                    I was very unhappy
EXAMPLE ___*F*___ ∧When we missed the Watermelon Festival last year.

_____ **1.** We all arrived early this year.

_____ **2.** It was going to be a busy day.

_____ **3.** Chose the events.

_____ **4.** When my little brother won the watermelon-seed-spitting contest.

_____ **5.** My dad entered the watermelon-eating contest.

_____ **6.** After eating nine slices.

_____ **7.** My best friend was crowned Watermelon Festival Queen.

_____ **8.** My mom won third place in the watermelon toss.

_____ **9.** When she was awarded her prize.

_____ **10.** Was a volunteer at the dunking booth.

_____ **11.** Because I dunked him four times.

_____ **12.** When my mom said I couldn't ride on the Screamer.

_____ **13.** While I was on the Whirling Hurricane.

_____ **14.** Rocky Road and the Detours at the festival.

_____ **15.** Because they are my favorite band.

Finding and Revising Fragments

DIRECTIONS Decide which of the following groups of words are sentence fragments.

- If the word group is a fragment, write *F*.
- Revise each fragment by (1) adding a subject, (2) adding a verb, or (3) attaching the fragment to a complete sentence. You may need to change the punctuation and capitalization, too.
- If the word group is already a complete sentence, write *S*.

EXAMPLE ___*F*___ After deciding to rent boats at the park ∧ *we were a little nervous* ⊙

_____ 1. None of us had ever been kayaking before.

_____ 2. A perfect day for a kayak trip down the North Fork River.

_____ 3. The fall air crisp and cool.

_____ 4. Falling from the trees along the banks.

_____ 5. A lot of equipment, such as lifejackets, fishing rods, and picnic supplies.

_____ 6. When we waded into the river to launch our kayaks.

_____ 7. Rainbow trout eating bugs off the surface of the water.

_____ 8. We found a good fishing spot.

_____ 9. Took pictures of all the fish we caught before we let them go.

_____ 10. Birds, squirrels, and even a snake.

_____ 11. Because we were getting hungry.

_____ 12. The sandwiches and salads.

_____ 13. While getting back into my kayak.

_____ 14. My splashing around made everyone laugh.

_____ 15. By the time we reached the end of our trip.

Identifying and Revising Run-on Sentences

DIRECTIONS Some of the following groups of words are run-on sentences.

- Revise each run-on by (1) making it into two separate sentences or (2) using a comma and *and*, *but*, or *or*.
- If the word group is already correct, write *C*.

EXAMPLE _____ I have always wanted a motorcycle ⌃and I'm saving up for one.

_____ **1.** Riding a motorcycle can be a lot of fun it can also be very dangerous.

_____ **2.** Motorcycles must share the road with cars and trucks these vehicles outweigh a motor-

cycle by several tons.

_____ **3.** Motorcycle riders must watch out for other hazards as well.

_____ **4.** Rain can make the surface of the road very slippery, loose gravel can cause a

motorcyclist to lose control.

_____ **5.** It's a good idea to take a course in motorcycle safety, courses are offered by many

police departments and motorcycle riders' associations.

_____ **6.** You'll learn the basics of operating a motorcycle, you'll learn how to react in

emergency situations.

_____ **7.** You'll also learn what kind of protective clothing you should wear when riding a

motorcycle.

_____ **8.** Many states require riders to protect their eyes, this protection keeps insects, stones,

and dust out of the eyes.

_____ **9.** You can wear motorcycle goggles, you can wear sunglasses.

_____ **10.** The Motorcycle Safety Foundation recommends a full-face helmet they say it is the

most important piece of safety equipment.

Identifying and Revising Run-on Sentences

DIRECTIONS Some of the following groups of words are run-on sentences.

- Revise each run-on by (1) making it into two separate sentences or (2) using a comma and *and, but,* or *or.*
- If the group of words is already correct, write *C.*

EXAMPLE _____ Caves are hollow areas in the earth, part of the definition of a cave is that

it is big enough to hold a person.

_____ **1.** A cave can be just large enough for one person it can be as huge as an enormous room.

_____ **2.** The largest known cave has 550 kilometers of passages, some think it has even more

unexplored areas.

_____ **3.** Limestone caves are common. They form when water dissolves the underground

limestone.

_____ **4.** Water remains in some caves, it forms deep underground lakes.

_____ **5.** One type of cave is formed when underground lava cools first on the outside the

molten lava inside then exits, leaving a hollow place.

_____ **6.** Crashing surf makes "sea caves," the water breaks down rock along the shore.

_____ **7.** A sinkhole is a cave with its entrance in the "roof," have you ever stumbled upon

a sinkhole?

_____ **8.** Stalactites and stalagmites are cave formations made from minerals deposited

by dripping water.

_____ **9.** Stalactites hang from the ceiling of a cave, stalagmites rise from its floor.

_____ **10.** These cave formations look like icicles and pillars individually, they form a column

from floor to ceiling when they connect.

Correcting Sentence Fragments and Run-ons

DIRECTIONS The following paragraph contains several sentence fragments
and run-on sentences.

- Underline the sentence fragments once and the run-on sentences twice.
- Rewrite the paragraph to eliminate the sentence fragments and correct
  the run-on sentences.
- Change the punctuation and capitalization as necessary to make each
  sentence clear and complete.

The human brain is made up of three main parts the three parts work
together to carry out complicated tasks. The cerebrum is where information
from your senses is processed. When your eyes see a skunk in the road. Your
cerebrum tells your arms to move the steering wheel to avoid it. The cerebellum controls balance and coordination, this is the part of the brain that helps
you hold a soft drink and change the radio station at the same time. When
you almost have a head-on collision from trying to do too many things at
once. The brain stem brings your heart rate back to normal.

_____

_____

_____

_____

_____

_____

_____

_____

_____

_____

_____

_____

_____

_____

Correcting Sentence Fragments and Run-ons

DIRECTIONS The following paragraph contains several sentence fragments and run-on sentences.

- Underline the sentence fragments once and the run-on sentences twice.
- Rewrite the paragraph to eliminate the sentence fragments and correct the run-on sentences.
- Change the punctuation and capitalization as necessary to make each sentence clear and complete.

The ancient Egyptians preserved the bodies of the dead with a special process of embalming the entire process took about seventy days. One of the first steps was removing the internal organs. Most of the organs taken out and placed in jars. A kind of rock salt was then used to dry the body. Once the body had dried completely. The Egyptians filled it with material to preserve its shape. Different materials were used. They packed the body with linen pads they filled it with sawdust. Next, the body was wrapped in many layers of linen bandages. When the wrapping was completed. The mummy was placed in a coffin. The ancient Egyptians' process very effective. Scientists sometimes unwrap mummies to study them. The bodies have deteriorated, you can still tell what the person looked like when he or she was alive.

_____

_____

_____

_____

_____

_____

_____

_____

_____

_____

_____

_____

Combining Sentences by Inserting Words

DIRECTIONS Each of the following items contains two sentences. To combine the two sentences, take the italicized key word from the second sentence and insert it into the first sentence. The directions in parentheses will tell you how to change the form of the key word if needed.

---

1. A horse is born ready to stand on its own legs. It has *four* legs.

_____

2. However, a kangaroo is born developed. Its development is *partial*. (Add *-ly*.)

_____

3. A newborn kangaroo must climb into its mother's pouch. The pouch is *warm*.

_____

4. The baby kangaroo grows in the pouch. The kangaroo grows *slowly*.

_____

5. The kangaroo will have large hind legs as an adult. Its legs will have a lot of *power*. (Add *-ful*.)

_____

6. Kangaroos use their hind legs to hop at speeds up to thirty miles per hour. They use the *strength* of their hind legs. (Change *strength* to *strong*.)

_____

_____

7. A kangaroo uses its tail for support and balance. It has a *long* tail.

_____

8. Kangaroos' ears can twist forward and backward. They *use* their ears constantly. (Add *-ful*.)

_____

9. Kangaroos are preyed upon by dogs called dingoes. These dogs live in *Australia*. (Change *Australia* to *Australian*.)

_____

10. Laws protect kangaroos from human hunters. These laws are *strict*.

_____

Combining Sentences by Inserting Words

DIRECTIONS Each of the following items contains two sentences. To combine the two sentences, take the italicized key word from the second sentence and insert it into the first sentence. The directions in parentheses will tell you how to change the form of the key word if needed.

1. Sleep is a state shared by human beings and animals. Sleep is *important.*

   _____

2. Scientists study people's habits. They study their habits when they *sleep.* (Add *-ing.*)

   _____

3. A sensitive machine can show how the brain functions during sleep. The machine's sensitivity is *high.* (Add *-ly.*)

   _____

4. Waking people's brains give off about ten electrical waves per second. The waves are *small.*

   _____

5. Brain waves continue during sleep. The brain waves *vary.* (Add *-ing.*)

   _____

6. People need both slow-moving and fast-moving brain waves for sleep. The sleep helps people *rest.* (Add *-ful.*)

   _____

7. People have eye movements when they experience fast-moving brain waves. The eye movements are *rapid.*

   _____

   _____

8. Dreams occur during REM (rapid eye movement) sleep. The dreams are *vivid.*

   _____

9. People sometimes question what their dreams mean. Their dreams *puzzle* them. (Add *-ing.*)

   _____

10. People who are prevented from entering deep sleep become irritable. It is an *eventual* result of missing deep sleep. (Add *-ly.*)

   _____

   _____

Combining Sentences by Inserting Phrases

DIRECTIONS Each of the following items contains two sentences. To combine the sentences, take the italicized word group from the second sentence and insert it into the first sentence. The hints in parentheses will tell you how to change the forms of words if needed.

1. Today, travelers can cross the United States in a matter of hours. They can do this *by airplane.*

   _____

2. The eight-thousand-mile journey of Meriwether Lewis and William Clark was no vacation. They were *the leaders of the Lewis and Clark expedition.*

   _____

3. President Thomas Jefferson sent a team of explorers westward. He *hoped to establish a route to the Pacific coast.* (Change *hoped* to *hoping.*)

   _____

4. In 1804, the group led by Lewis and Clark set out from St. Louis on its journey. It was *to explore the northwestern region.*

   _____

5. The explorers had problems from the very beginning of the journey. They *had to paddle their heavy boats upstream against the swift current of the Missouri River.* (Change *had* to *having.*)

   _____

6. The explorers tried to establish good relations with the Native Americans they met. They *gave them presents.* (Change *gave* to *by giving.*)

   _____

7. Many people the explorers met were friendly. They were *eager to offer food and advice.*

   _____

8. Sacagawea joined the expedition team as an interpreter. She was *a Shoshone woman.*

   _____

9. The team began a very difficult part of its journey. They *crossed the Bitterroot Mountains.* (Change *crossed* to *after crossing.*)

   _____

10. When they reached the Pacific Ocean, they built a fort where they spent the winter. There they *gathered strength for their long trip home.* (Change *gathered* to *gathering.*)

    _____

Combining Sentences by Inserting Phrases

DIRECTIONS Each of the following items contains two sentences. To combine the sentences, take the italicized word group from the second sentence and insert it into the first sentence. The hints in parentheses will tell you how to change the forms of words if needed.

1. Many animals migrate from the place where they were born. They migrate *to find food or better living conditions.*

   _____

2. Some animals make one great journey in their lifetime. They are *like the Pacific salmon.*

   _____

3. Salmon are born in freshwater streams but live most of their adult lives in the ocean. They *return upstream to spawn.* (Change *return* to *returning.*)

   _____

4. After spawning, the Pacific salmon dies. It *has completed its life cycle.* (Change *has completed* to *having completed.*)

   _____

5. Other animals migrate annually. They *make a round-trip journey.* (Change *make* to *making.*)

   _____

6. Some birds go south for the winter. They *sense the change of seasons.* (Change *sense* to *sensing.*)

   _____

7. Scientists believe that a bird's "inner calendar" tells it when to return home in the spring. The inner calendar is *present at birth.*

   _____

8. The arctic tern is one of the record holders for long-distance migrations. It *travels up to 22,000 miles in a year.* (Change *travels* to *traveling.*)

   _____

9. Adult humpback whales spend most of their time where their food supply is most abundant. They live *in the icy water of the polar regions.*

   _____

10. When a female whale is ready to give birth, she and her mate migrate to warmer tropical waters. They migrate *for the sake of the newborn calf.*

   _____

Creating Compound Subjects and Verbs

DIRECTIONS Combine each of the following pairs of short, choppy sentences by using *and*, *but*, or *or*.
- If the two sentences have the same verb, make a compound subject.
- If they have the same subject, make a compound verb.

1. Toads belong to a group of animals called amphibians. Frogs belong to a group of animals called amphibians.

   _____

2. Amphibians can survive in the water. Amphibians can live on land.

   _____

3. Female toads can lay thousands of eggs at a time. Female frogs can lay thousands of eggs at a time.

   _____

4. Tadpoles hatch from the eggs. Tadpoles remain in the water as they mature into adult frogs.

   _____

   _____

5. Toads do not like direct sunlight. Toads are most active during rainy days or at night.

   _____

6. People do not get warts from toads. People may get sick from touching a toad's back.

   _____

7. Toads burrow to escape extreme weather. Toads hibernate to escape extreme weather.

   _____

8. Frogs are beneficial to humans because they eat insect pests. Toads are beneficial to humans for the same reason.

   _____

   _____

9. The cane toad is one of the largest toads. The cane toad can grow up to nine inches in length.

   _____

10. The Goliath frog of West Africa is the largest frog. The Goliath frog weighs about seven pounds.

   _____

Creating Compound Subjects and Verbs

DIRECTIONS Combine each of the following pairs of short, choppy sentences
by using *and, but,* or *or.*

- If the two sentences have the same verb, make a compound subject.
- If they have the same subject, make a compound verb.

1. Alligators are reptiles. Crocodiles are reptiles.

   _____

2. Both animals' eyes sit high on their heads. Both animals' eyes let them see above water.

   _____

3. Crocodiles use their short, strong legs for walking on land. Crocodiles swim by moving their tails from side to side.

   _____

4. A crocodile looks much like an alligator. A crocodile weighs only about two-thirds as much as an alligator.

   _____

5. Crocodiles eat small animals such as fish and birds. Crocodiles occasionally attack large animals and people.

   _____

6. Alligators have long snouts and sharp teeth. Crocodiles have long snouts and sharp teeth.

   _____

7. An alligator's snout is long. An alligator's snout is broader and more rounded than a crocodile's snout.

   _____

8. Crocodiles hide their eggs in nests of brush or leaves. Crocodiles bury their eggs in the sand.

   _____

9. Crocodiles were once widely hunted for their hides. Alligators were once widely hunted for their hides.

   _____

10. Alligators were once classified as an endangered species. Alligators have been reclassified because their numbers are increasing.

    _____

    _____

Forming Compound Sentences

DIRECTIONS Each of the following pairs of sentences is closely related.
Make each pair a compound sentence by adding a comma and a coordinating
conjunction such as *and* or *but*.

EXAMPLE The Sahara is almost as big as the United States, but It has only two million inhabitants.

1. This desert has one of the world's harshest climates. Large portions of it are completely uninhabited.

2. The word *Sahara* comes from the Arabic word for desert. Different parts of this desert have other names.

3. The Sahara contains valuable minerals such as copper, iron, tin, and gold. Many of these have not yet been mined.

4. The Saharan climate is hot and dry. The air turns cool at night.

5. Much of the desert consists of vast seas of sand called *ergs*. The shifting sand in these ergs can form dunes as high as 600 feet.

6. The landscape of the Sahara does not change for mile after mile. This is probably why it is nicknamed "ocean of the sands."

7. People believe that a continuous sandy landscape is typical of the Sahara. This terrain accounts for only one-eighth of the desert's area.

8. The Painted Desert in Arizona differs in character from the Sahara. Its name indicates its more colorful terrain.

9. Its brightly colored rocks impressed a U.S. government explorer. He chose the name "painted" to describe the place.

10. Navajo and Hopi reservations are part of the Painted Desert. The Navajo use the colorful sands to make ceremonial paintings.

Forming Compound Sentences

DIRECTIONS Each of the following pairs of sentences is closely related.
Make each pair a compound sentence by adding a comma and a coordinating
conjunction such as *and* or *but*.

EXAMPLE Pompeii was an ancient city in Italy. It was buried under the ashes of a

volcanic eruption in A.D. 79.

1. Earthquakes damaged the ancient city in A.D. 62. It was a volcanic eruption that ultimately

destroyed Pompeii.

2. Pompeii was not famous in its time. It is better known today because its ruins are so well

preserved.

3. Mount Vesuvius erupted violently in the summer of A.D. 79. Pompeii was engulfed in hot

ashes and poisonous gases.

4. When the ashes fell on Pompeii, much of the city was buried. Only columns and rooftops

were left visible.

5. Survivors recovered some valuables that they had left behind in the city. Later eruptions

buried any remaining items.

6. Almost 1,400 years later, people knew of the buried city. No one paid much attention to it.

7. In 1748, a man was digging in a vineyard. His shovel hit a buried wall.

8. Italian historians were excited by the discovery. Archaeologists soon began to excavate, hoping

to find important artifacts.

9. Archaeologists decided to leave many objects where they were found. They began restoring

the site to its original condition.

10. After ongoing excavation, about three-fourths of Pompeii is visible. Visitors can see how the

Pompeians lived.

PRACTICE A, WORKSHEET 17

Using Subordinate Clauses

DIRECTIONS Combine the pair of sentences into one.

- Make the second sentence a subordinate clause and attach it to the first sentence, following the clues given.
- You may need to cut a word or two from the second sentence.

....

EXAMPLE The banjo is an instrument. ~~This instrument~~ *that* became popular in the United States in the nineteenth century.

1. A banjo is a stringed musical instrument. It combines a guitar neck with a body like a tambourine. (Use *that*.)

2. The banjo was developed in Africa. It was brought to America. (Use *before*.)

3. The body of the banjo is covered with animal skin or plastic. The material is stretched over a round frame. (Use *that*.)

4. This body gives the banjo its characteristic sound. Its strings are plucked. (Use *when*.)

5. A five-string banjo's shortest string is fastened to a screw in the neck. This string is known as the "thumb string." (Use *which*.)

6. My sister decided to play the banjo. She listened to a famous banjo picker. (Use *after*.)

7. She has become an enthusiastic banjo student. She practices night and day. (Use *who*.)

8. Fingerpicking is a style of banjo playing. It is said to "sparkle." (Use *that*.)

9. My sister is good at frailing. Frailing is a way of strumming the banjo instead of picking it. (Use *which*.)

10. People cannot help but dance. Banjo players start strumming and picking. (Use *when*.)

Using Subordinate Clauses

DIRECTIONS Combine the pair of sentences into one.

- Make the second sentence a subordinate clause and attach it to the first sentence, following the clues given.
- You may need to cut a word or two from the second sentence.

EXAMPLE Newfoundland is an eastern Canadian province. ~~It~~ *that* is not heavily populated.

1. John Cabot, an Italian, discovered Newfoundland in 1497. Cabot explored for England.

   (Use *who*.)

2. He spread the word about the area. Fish were plentiful there. (Use *where*.)

3. Many fishing boats came from different countries. People heard the news. (Use *after*.)

4. Fishing crews competed for the area. They knew the area could supply a lot of food.

   (Use *which*.)

5. Communities of fishing camps existed for many years. The area finally became a colony in

   1824. (Use *before*.)

6. Its people showed their strong independence. They refused to become Canadians until 1949.

   (Use *when*.)

7. Part of Newfoundland is an island. It is separated from the mainland by the Strait of Belle Isle.

   (Use *that*.)

8. The rest of Newfoundland is made up of the Labrador coast. This coast is part of the Canadian

   mainland. (Use *which*.)

9. Newfoundland's largest city is St. John's. St. John's is also the capital of the province.

   (Use *which*.)

10. The area has a wild, rugged seacoast. It stretches for 10,000 miles. (Use *that*.)

Revising a Paragraph by Combining Sentences

DIRECTIONS The following paragraph sounds choppy because it has too many short sentences. Use the methods you have learned in the "Combining Sentences" section to combine sentences in the paragraph.

- First, mark up the paragraph to show the revisions you will make.
- Then, rewrite the paragraph.

Atlantic puffins are seabirds. Atlantic puffins nest along northern seacoasts. They spend most of their adult lives far out at sea. They come to land only to nest. The parents dig a hole in the ground three to six feet deep. The female usually lays one white egg. Both adults incubate it for more than a month. The chick hatches. It stays warm under its parents' wings for a few days. Puffins can be identified by their bright beaks. They can be identified by their multi-colored beaks. "Sea parrot" is one nickname for these colorful birds. "Clown of the sea" is another nickname for them. "Bottlenose" is a third nickname. They are clumsy fliers. They are graceful and efficient swimmers. They propel themselves with their wings. They use their feet to steer. Puffins are comical in appearance. Puffins are talented fishers.

_____

_____

_____

_____

_____

_____

_____

_____

_____

_____

_____

Revising a Paragraph by Combining Sentences

DIRECTIONS The following paragraph sounds choppy because it has too
many short sentences. Use the methods you have learned in the "Combining
Sentences" section to combine sentences in the paragraph.

- First, mark up the paragraph to show the revisions you will make.
- Then, rewrite the paragraph.

Gray meerkats are a type of mongoose. Gray meerkats live in the Kalahari

Desert in southern Africa. Gray meerkats travel in groups. Gray meerkats

hunt for insects during the day. Meerkats are small. Meerkats are often hunted

by birds of prey. Meerkats have to dig for insects. They cannot watch for

predators at the same time. For this reason, some meerkats hunt. Others stand

guard. The guards take their job very seriously. The guards stay on constant

lookout for danger. Later, other meerkats stand watch. The guards get a

chance to eat. Cooperation is necessary for survival. Alone, meerkats are more

vulnerable.

_____

_____

_____

_____

_____

_____

_____

_____

_____

_____

_____

_____

_____

_____

Revising Stringy Sentences

DIRECTIONS Some of the following sentences are stringy and need to be improved.

- Revise them by (1) breaking each sentence into two or more sentences or
  (2) turning some of the complete thoughts into phrases or subordinate clauses.
- If the sentence is effective and does not need to be improved, write *C* for *correct*.

EXAMPLE _____ When Lightning streaks across the sky, ~~and~~ many people are fascinated.

_____ **1.** Lightning is one of the most beautiful and spectacular events in nature.

_____ **2.** Lightning can also be deadly, and lightning kills about 100 Americans every year.

_____ **3.** Benjamin Franklin used a kite to help prove that lightning was made of electricity, but his experiment was very dangerous, and Franklin was lucky that he was not killed.

_____ **4.** The safest place to be during an electrical storm is inside a building, or you can also take shelter inside a car, but be careful not to touch any of the metal parts.

_____ **5.** Lightning can travel through telephone lines, and lightning can strike people through the phone, and because of this you should not use a telephone during a thunderstorm.

_____ **6.** Lightning often strikes water, and it is dangerous to be in a pool during a thunderstorm, and that is why lifeguards clear the pool when they see lightning.

_____ **7.** Since lightning usually strikes the tallest object in an area, it is dangerous to stand in an open field, on top of a hill, or on a beach during a thunderstorm.

_____ **8.** Standing under a tall tree during a thunderstorm is not a good idea, and if lightning strikes the tree, it can jump from the tree to nearby objects.

Revising Stringy Sentences

DIRECTIONS Some of the following sentences are stringy and need to be improved.

- Revise them by (1) breaking each sentence into two or more sentences or
  (2) turning some of the complete thoughts into phrases or subordinate clauses.
- If the sentence is effective and does not need to be improved, write *C* for *correct*.

EXAMPLE _____ People like to change styles and one way they do this is by changing their hair.

_____ **1.** Our hair does much more than keep our ears warm, and it can have a big effect on

how we feel about ourselves, and it can be used to express our individuality.

_____ **2.** We think our hair looks good, and we feel more confident, and we feel able to face

the world.

_____ **3.** All it takes is one bad haircut to make a person want to flee from society and hide

under a bed until his or her hair grows out, and this can take a long time, since hair

grows only about half an inch a month.

_____ **4.** Hair can be changed with a snip of the scissors, and hair can also be changed by

curling, straightening, or dyeing.

_____ **5.** We can do so many different things with our hair, and because of this our hairstyles

become a mode of self-expression, and people often make statements about who they

are by how they style their hair.

_____ **6.** Hardly any other part of our physical appearance can be changed as easily as our hair.

_____ **7.** Some people like to do the opposite of what "everyone" is doing, and they wear

unique hairstyles, and their hairstyles set them apart from the crowd.

_____ **8.** Styles are as unique and individualized as the people wearing them, and different

styles make the world more interesting.

Revising Wordy Sentences

DIRECTIONS Some of the following sentences are wordy and need improvement.

- Decide which sentences are wordy and revise them. You can (1) replace a phrase with one word, (2) take out *who is* or *which is*, or (3) take out a whole group of unnecessary words.
- If a sentence is effective as it is, write *C* for *correct*.

EXAMPLE _____ Place a new toy in front of a baby and ~~see~~ what happens, watching what the baby does with the new toy.

_____ **1.** Being very curious, the baby will use all five of its senses to explore the new toy.

_____ **2.** Our ancestors probably explored the world in much the same way, which is to say, using their senses to gain knowledge about their environment.

_____ **3.** However, as far as learning about the moon was concerned, the moon was too far away for people to explore with any sense except sight.

_____ **4.** Because of the fact that the moon changed, it was a natural subject for stories.

_____ **5.** The Greeks and Romans thought that the moon was a goddess with three faces.

_____ **6.** Early scientists offered a variety of explanations about life on the moon, and in fact, one scientist wrote that he believed the craters were built by moon creatures.

_____ **7.** In 1609, Galileo, who was an Italian astronomer, became the first person to study the moon with a telescope.

_____ **8.** Some people who were writers imagined traveling to the moon using antigravity devices or huge cannons to propel them.

_____ **9.** The first moon landing, which took place in 1969, provided scientists with new information about the moon.

_____ **10.** The astronauts brought back samples of rocks from the moon, proving completely and beyond a shadow of a doubt that the moon is NOT made of cheese.

Revising Wordy Sentences

DIRECTIONS Some of the following sentences are wordy and need improvement.

■ Decide which sentences are wordy and revise them. You can (1) replace a phrase with one word, (2) take out *who is* or *which is,* or (3) take out a whole group of unnecessary words.

■ If a sentence is effective as it is, write *C* for *correct.*

EXAMPLE _____ For some people, watching fish ~~swimming around~~ in ~~the water of~~ an aquarium

is just not enough.

_____ **1.** These people, who are eager to learn for themselves about aquatic life firsthand, would

climb right into the aquarium if they could.

_____ **2.** This desire to explore the world of fish and aquatic plants that live underwater gave

birth to the sport of scuba diving.

_____ **3.** Scuba diving, which is a relatively new sport, is becoming more and more popular.

_____ **4.** Throughout the course of history, people have been diving in search of fish, shells, and

treasure.

_____ **5.** Up until the time at which scuba gear was invented, divers could stay underwater for

only as long as they could hold their breath.

_____ **6.** Some could stay under as long as three minutes, but this was dangerous because of

the fact that divers can pass out underwater, endangering their lives.

_____ **7.** Learning how to operate scuba gear requires lessons from a certified scuba instructor.

_____ **8.** Public swimming pools and colleges sometimes offer courses of instruction that teach

people to scuba dive.

_____ **9.** In a scuba-diving course, you will learn that you should never go out on your own and

scuba dive by yourself.

_____ **10.** You will also learn how to avoid dangerous sea creatures that can harm you as a diver.

Adding Variety to Sentences

DIRECTIONS The following paragraph is uninteresting because it includes only compound sentences.

■ Rewrite the paragraph to include a variety of sentence structures.

■ In your version mix short, simple sentences; compound sentences; and longer sentences with subordinate clauses.

To become a fly fisher, you must master certain skills, and you must learn a lot about fish. You have to learn how to assemble your fly rod, and you must learn how to cast. You must cast the fly so that it drops onto the water like a snowflake, and you have to prevent the fishing line from slapping the water. It might not sound difficult, but novice fly fishers often spend hours untangling fishing line. You also need to learn where to find fish, and you must find out what these fish eat. It can all seem like a lot of work just to catch a fish, and the work can be hard. Catching that first beautiful trout makes all the work feel worthwhile, and you will think you found the gold at the end of the rainbow!

_____

_____

_____

_____

_____

_____

_____

_____

_____

_____

_____

_____

_____

_____

_____

_____

_____

_____

_____

Adding Variety to Sentences

DIRECTIONS The following paragraph is uninteresting because it includes only compound sentences.

- Rewrite the paragraph to include a variety of sentence structures.
- In your version mix short simple sentences; compound sentences; and longer sentences with subordinate clauses.

    Earth seems to be "solid as a rock," but its outer shell is actually made of rocky plates. The plates slide past each other slowly, and sometimes they collide. This creates great pressure on the outer edges of the plates, and this pressure builds up greatly. The rocks break under the strain and this creates an earthquake. The land that rings the Pacific Ocean is called the "Ring of Fire" and that is where most earthquakes occur. The largest earthquakes in the United States were in New Madrid, Missouri, and these occurred in the early 1800s. The largest of these New Madrid earthquakes was felt from Canada to the Gulf of Mexico, and this earthquake changed the course of the Mississippi River.

_____

_____

_____

_____

_____

_____

_____

_____

_____

_____

_____

_____

_____

_____

_____

_____

_____

_____

_____

_____

Revise a Paragraph by Improving Sentence Style

DIRECTIONS The following paragraph is hard to read because it contains stringy and wordy sentences.

- Revise the paragraph using the methods you have learned.
- Try to mix simple, compound, and complex sentences in your improved version.

Who can forget the thrill of the first time when you learned to ride a bicycle? However, the fact of the matter is that the thrill wears off as bicycles become our main transportation. As a result of what happens when we get older, once we get our driver's licenses, we don't even use our bicycles. Our bicycles are stored away in the garage, and they serve no purpose, and all they do is gather dust. Now, though, due to the fact that the mountain bike was developed, people are rediscovering the enjoyment and pleasure of biking that they first experienced as children. With its sturdy frame and knobby tires, the mountain bike is luring adults out to play, and it has brought bicyclists out in force to embrace and explore the land beyond the pavement. Mountain-bike trails wind through the nation's parks and wilderness areas and help adults satisfy the need to play and explore, which never really goes away and which stays with them forever.

_____

_____

_____

_____

_____

_____

_____

_____

_____

_____

_____

_____

_____

_____

_____

_____

Revise a Paragraph by Improving Sentence Style

DIRECTIONS The following paragraph is hard to read because it contains stringy and wordy sentences.

- Revise the paragraph using the methods you have learned.
- Try to mix simple, compound, and complex sentences in your improved version.

....

   A dollar bill is just a piece of paper and has no value in and of itself and isn't worth anything. Dollar bills, as well as coins, checks, and credit cards, have value because we all agree that they have value. Before money was invented, people had to trade what they had for what they wanted, which was a system that was much less convenient than paying with money. This was known as the barter system, and people traded animal hides, cloth, animals, or other goods and services to get what they wanted, but the system did not always work. What if you went to the market to trade your goat for some chickens, and the person who had chickens to trade already had enough goats, and you would have to go home without a chicken? This problem is solved when there is an agreed-upon monetary system approved by society, providing a solution to the problems of the barter system. People accept money for the reason that they know that they can use the money to buy many different things. It's hard to imagine a world without some kind of monetary system. If money had never been invented, would people have to take along a couple of goats to the shopping mall when they went shopping instead of credit cards?

_____

_____

_____

_____

_____

_____

_____

_____

_____

_____

_____

_____

_____

_____

_____

Identifying Main Ideas and Topic Sentences

DIRECTIONS Look for the main idea in each of the following paragraphs. Remember that the main idea is the overall point of the paragraph.

- If the selection has a topic sentence, underline it.
- If there is no topic sentence, write the main idea of the paragraph in your own words, using details from the paragraph.

1. Many people know an orca when they see one. Orcas have distinct black-and-white markings that make them easy to recognize. Commonly known as killer whales, they are a popular subject for documentaries and feature films. Frequently, orcas are featured performers in aquatic shows. Perhaps no other sea mammal is as familiar to people.

Main idea: _____

2. There are some common misconceptions about orcas. For one thing, they are not, as some people think, the largest species of whale. The orca is merely the largest member of the dolphin family of whales. Furthermore, many people think of orcas as solitary creatures, but they usually live in groups of up to fifty animals.

Main idea: _____

3. Killer whales hunt in organized groups. Working together, a group of killer whales can herd prey animals into shallow water, trapping them against the shore. Orcas' speed and body shape are ideal for hunting. Large, strong teeth and powerful jaw muscles help them seize large prey. Although they usually feed on fish and squid, they have been known to hunt successfully animals as large as great whales.

Main idea: _____

4. Orcas were once called whale killers, but the name has somehow been transposed to *killer whales*. Orcas are called killers not because of their behavior toward humans, but because of the way they treat other ocean creatures. They are fierce, quick, and intelligent predators with huge appetites. Orcas will hunt fish, squid, penguins, seals, whales, and other dolphins. Nonetheless, there are no records of an orca killing a human.

Main idea: _____

Writing a Topic Sentence

DIRECTIONS For each of the following paragraphs, write a topic sentence that communicates the main idea.

1. Before 1966, the ice axes used in mountain climbing had straight blades. This limited the kinds of slopes that could be climbed. When Yvon Chouinard added a slight curve to the pick side of the ax, however, even the steepest slopes seemed attainable. It was, indeed, the beginning of a new sport called *ice climbing.*

Topic sentence: _____

2. The curved ice ax has allowed climbers to take on nearly vertical slopes that once seemed impossible. Now, armed with their axes, daring ice climbers prefer the extremely dangerous vertical slopes. Some of their favorite challenges are frozen waterfalls.

Topic sentence: _____

3. Frozen waterfalls are intensely beautiful. Climbing on such ice is like climbing on a diamond that sparkles blue one minute and yellow the next. In addition, ice climbers get a breathtaking view of the winter world below them. Ice climbers also enjoy the challenges of frozen waterfalls. All the challenges of climbing an entire mountain can be encountered by scaling a single frozen waterfall.

Topic sentence: _____

4. When ice climbers are on the side of a frozen waterfall, their arms and legs are in constant use. Each hand holds an ice ax. Strapped to each boot are crampons, which are a layer of two-inch spikes, some of which point forward to grip the ice. It takes strength to drive the ax into the ice. Even when a climber is not moving, each muscle is needed to hold on.

Topic sentence: _____

5. Many experienced mountain and rock climbers shy away from this dramatic and dangerous sport. Those who do attempt the sport of ice climbing tend to be well prepared. They must have the right boots, gloves, spikes, and other equipment. While climbing, they are very slow and careful.

Topic sentence: _____

Collecting Supporting Details

DIRECTIONS When you write paragraphs, you have to collect details that support your main idea. Practice with the following topic sentences. On the lines provided, list at least two details to support each topic sentence.

1. If I could organize a field trip, I know just where we would go.

   Details: _____

   _____

2. I have accomplished something important.

   Details: _____

   _____

3. Here is a person whom I consider successful.

   Details: _____

   _____

4. I'm the kind of person who says what I think.

   Details: _____

   _____

5. Cars have changed a lot since the 1970's.

   Details: _____

   _____

6. Last summer was different from all the summers before it.

   Details: _____

   _____

7. I hope to have an unusual career someday.

   Details: _____

   _____

8. I think everyone needs a pet.

   Details: _____

   _____

Developing a Clincher Sentence

DIRECTIONS For each of the following short paragraphs, write a sentence that can serve as its clincher, wrapping up the information presented in the paragraph, but not repeating it.

1. What animal is most closely associated with cold climates? It's probably the penguin. This is understandable because most penguins do live in very cold places, including the Antarctic. Some types of penguins, however, can tolerate warmer climates. One species even lives at the equator.

Clincher sentence: _____

2. There are several species of penguins, but a casual observer might not be able to tell them apart. One of the biggest differences is in their height and weight; they range from just over one foot tall and weighing two pounds to nearly four feet tall and weighing ninety pounds. Otherwise, they look basically the same. All are black and white, though some have tufts of yellow on their brow, and a few have streaks of yellow or orange on their upper body.

Clincher sentence: _____

3. Penguins cannot fly, of course, and from a distance they look as if they do not even have feathers. They do, however, have soft, downy feathers that keep them warm. They molt, or lose their feathers, once a year. While they are molting, they cannot go in the water. They stay in a sheltered area with other molting penguins.

Clincher sentence: _____

4. Their wings function as flippers; they use them to "fly" underwater. Penguins are efficient swimmers, and they are great fun to watch. When they are moving really fast, they leap out of the water to breathe, sometimes soaring three feet or more through the air.

Clincher sentence: _____

5. They are also fun to watch on land. They seem to waddle around but can move quite fast. On their home turf, they have to navigate their way around ice and rocks. Sometimes a penguin will flop on its belly and slide along, using its feet and wings to keep going.

Clincher sentence: _____

Identifying Sentences That Destroy Unity

DIRECTIONS Each of the following paragraphs has one sentence that destroys the unity. Cross out the unrelated sentence.

....

1. The atmosphere on Venus is made up mostly of carbon dioxide and is heavier than the atmosphere on any other known planet. The average atmospheric pressure on Venus is ninety times greater than the average pressure on Earth's surface. Venus is the second planet from the Sun. If you stood on the surface of Venus, the amount of pressure on your body would be similar to the amount of pressure you would feel if you stood more than half a mile underwater on Earth.

2. Venus also experiences extreme temperatures. Venus is named for the goddess of love. The upper atmosphere goes from warm to extremely cold; it can vary from 25 degrees centigrade in the day to –150 degrees centigrade at night. The temperature increases, however, in the lower atmosphere. The planet's surface is unspeakably hot. It is hot enough to melt lead.

3. Venus's atmosphere is made up of thick clouds. Several layers of clouds surround the entire planet, and the layers move at different rates. The planet was called Phosphorus. The upper cloud layers move very rapidly, while the lower layers move more slowly. In fact, the upper clouds move about one hundred times faster than the lowest clouds.

4. Venus's cloudy atmosphere and extreme temperatures are related. The clouds that cover the planet reflect a lot of heat, so Venus absorbs less heat than Earth does. The heat that is absorbed is trapped and intensified by the clouds, and the surface temperature climbs. Radar images suggest that Venus may have sand dunes.

5. In the past, the dense cloud cover and turbulent atmosphere have made it difficult to see what the surface of Venus looks like. Venus rotates once every 243 Earth days. Scientists have been able to explore Venus, however. They have used spacecraft and radar to photograph and map the planet's surface.

Arranging Details by Using Chronological Order

DIRECTIONS Follow the directions for each item to practice telling about events
in the order in which they happen.

1. **Tell a story.** Circle one of the following topics, and make up three or more events to include
   in a story about it. List the events in chronological order.

   - You have been assigned as supervisor to a group of eight-year-olds at an event.
   - It was an ordinary Monday until the principal announced that the school mascot was
     missing.
   - The room was an absolute wreck, and your parents were due to be home in two hours.
     You asked yourself, "How did I get into this mess?"

   Events:

   a. _____

   _____

   b. _____

   _____

   c. _____

   _____

2. **Explain a process.** Circle one of the following activities. Then, list three or more steps involved
   in performing this activity. Arrange the steps in chronological order—that is, the order in which
   they should happen.

   - directing a visitor to the school cafeteria from your classroom
   - folding a paper airplane
   - teaching a dog a trick

   Steps:

   a. _____

   _____

   b. _____

   _____

   c. _____

   _____

for **EXERCISE 7**   *page 301*   **WORKSHEET 35**

Arranging Details by Using Spatial Order

DIRECTIONS For each subject in the chart, list descriptive details and then arrange the details in spatial order.

▶ LIST OF DETAILS	▶ DETAILS IN SPATIAL ORDER
1. the most interesting landscapes you have ever seen	
2. your favorite place for doing homework	
3. the perfect clothes for hiking	
4. the oddest pet you have ever seen	
5. the most unusual motor vehicle you have ever come across	

Arranging Details by Using Logical Order

DIRECTIONS For each set of subjects in the chart, write down three ways that the two are alike and three ways that they are different.

▶ TOPIC	▶ ALIKE	▶ DIFFERENT
1. vegetables and dessert	1. 2. 3.	1. 2. 3.
2. music your parents like and music you like	1. 2. 3.	1. 2. 3.
3. fun time with family and fun time with friends	1. 2. 3.	1. 2. 3.
4. team sports and individual sports	1. 2. 3.	1. 2. 3.
5. having a pet dog and having a pet goldfish	1. 2. 3.	1. 2. 3.

Identifying Transitional Words and Phrases

DIRECTIONS Underline all of the transitional words and phrases in the following paragraphs.

1. "It's going to storm," warned Grandmother, pointing to birds way up in the afternoon sky. Only a few clouds were in sight, but I knew she was right. When a thunderstorm is forming, warm, moist air flows upward. Consequently, flying insects are drawn up, too. Because the insects are higher, birds must fly higher than usual to catch and eat them. As a result, the birds provide a sign that the atmosphere is right for developing thunderstorms. The swallows we saw were flying so high that we could barely see them. Grandmother and I therefore checked the TV weather forecast, and just as Grandmother thought, rain was expected.

2. Do you think crayons are just for little kids? Think again. Just about everyone, from preschoolers to professional artists, loves crayons. Crayons are so popular, in fact, that some clubs work to preserve their history. In 1991, for example, these clubs protested when several old crayon colors were replaced with new, updated colors. In addition to liking the colors themselves, people like the expressive names of some crayons, such as *plum jam* for purple. People are also crazy about the scent of crayons. For example, their waxy smell is one of the top twenty scents recognized by adults. Clearly, crayons are not just for kids!

3. Add together a cloudless night, a group of campers, and several tele-scopes, and what do you have? A star party, of course. Star parties take place at national parks, state campgrounds, and observatories—anywhere far from light sources such as cities. The night sky has to be very dark for the stars to show up well. Before the party begins, a park ranger or astronomer explains which constellations or planets are visible at that time of year. When darkness finally arrives, the Milky Way splashes its 200 billion stars across the sky, and it's time for the party to begin. Campers step up to telescopes and focus. Suddenly, Saturn's rings seem huge and bright. The moon's craters look truly deep. When the stars begin to fade around dawn, campers stumble into tents to sleep all day.

Elaborating Details

DIRECTIONS The following paragraphs do not have enough elaboration. Rewrite each paragraph, adding details, facts, or examples to improve it.

1. Setting up a successful trip to the mall can be harder than it seems. First, you have to decide whether to go alone or with friends. Next, there is the matter of getting there. Most important, you have to have a good game plan about how to spend your time there.

_____

_____

_____

_____

2. It is really very easy to tell good movies from bad ones. Good movies have an interesting story and are fun to watch. Bad movies might have one or two good points, but when they are over, you find yourself saying, "Boy, that was stupid."

_____

_____

_____

_____

3. Families should prepare themselves for the possibility of extreme weather. Sometimes weather conditions result in a lack of electricity and water. It can even be hard to get fresh food. If people were prepared, then extreme weather would not seem like such a problem.

_____

_____

_____

_____

Identifying Types of Paragraphs

DIRECTIONS Answer the questions for each paragraph below.

1. This kitten has been in our house for only three weeks, but already it seems to belong to everyone. I always thought my brother Emil was my ally, but last night he proved me wrong. I heard meows and giggles coming from his room and went to investigate. I did not see them at first, but as I came around the bed I noticed the closet door was ajar. I opened it and there were the kitten and Emil, playing with my favorite ball!

Is this paragraph narrative, descriptive, expository, or persuasive? _____

How can you tell? _____

_____

2. So tell me, why would anyone want a kitten? Cats have absolutely no intelligence. An animal with real intelligence knows how to fetch things like newspapers and balls. Cats require too much equipment, like litter boxes and scratching posts. Worst of all, they have no sense of loyalty. They rarely come when they are called. I say people should stick to nice, reliable pets such as dogs. I ought to know; I am one.

Is this paragraph narrative, descriptive, expository, or persuasive? _____

How can you tell? _____

_____

3. Did you ever pay attention to cats' history? The earliest available records indicate that the Egyptians probably were the first to try to domesticate cats. Cats also appear in the art and literature of ancient cultures in Greece, Crete, China, and India. They were domesticated to keep rat populations down, and they have retained their hunting instinct. It is likely that they have always been self-reliant.

Is this paragraph narrative, descriptive, expository, or persuasive? _____

How can you tell? _____

_____

Dividing a Piece into Paragraphs

DIRECTIONS The passage that follows was originally broken into five paragraphs.

■ Indicate where you think the paragraph breaks went—or should go—by underlining the first word of each paragraph.

■ Then, explain your choices.

....

Have you ever been to a kite-flying contest? If you have, then you know that there are lots of unique and unusual kites being flown today. Kites come in all shapes and sizes and can be made with many different kinds of materials. Most people are familiar with the fairly simple diamond-shaped kites made of wooden sticks and paper. Kites, however, may be made of cloth or plastic and may be shaped like rectangles, triangles, squares, or even hexagons. Kites get their name from a bird called a kite. This hawklike bird glides on air currents while searching for prey. When it sees a mouse or an insect, it suddenly swerves, dips, or soars upward, chasing its prey. In a similar manner, a kite flown by people hovers in the sky and, with the jerk of a string, dives with a sudden whoosh or dances wildly across the sky. People in Asia have been flying kites as far back as recorded history. In some countries, such as China, Japan, Korea, and Malaysia, kite flying is a national pastime. Kites have symbolic significance in some of these countries and are flown on ceremonial occasions. An American famous for kite flying is Ben Franklin. According to legend, he hung a metal key on his kite line and flew the kite in a thunderstorm. As Franklin reportedly expected, the key attracted electricity from the air, providing evidence that lightning is electrical in nature. Because most people do not wish to be struck by lightning, modern kite flyers should think of Franklin's experience as a lesson about kite-flying conditions to avoid. Bad weather certainly can be dangerous to kite flyers, but it is not the only threat. Electrical wires can also be very hazardous. The best way to fly a kite is on a clear day, out in the open. The wind should be strong enough to keep the kite in the air, but not so strong that it will tear the kite to pieces. Ideally the wind should be between eight and twenty miles an hour. Never fly a kite in damp weather or near power lines.

Explanation for paragraph breaks:

_____

_____

_____

_____

Answer Key

Grading Scale

The exercises generally contain ten numbered items.
To facilitate grading, the chart below shows the
number of points per item in exercises containing
different numbers of items.

Number of Items in Exercise	Number of Points per Item to Total 100
3	33.3
5	20
6	16.7
8	12.5
15	6.66
20	5

Answer Key

Chapter 8

Writing Effective Sentences

p. 1 | **Exercise 1**
PRACTICE A, Worksheet 1

1. F		**11.** S	
2. F		**12.** F	
3. S		**13.** S	
4. F		**14.** F	
5. F		**15.** F	
6. F		**16.** F	
7. F		**17.** F	
8. S		**18.** S	
9. F		**19.** F	
10. F		**20.** F	

p. 2 | **Exercise 1**
PRACTICE B, Worksheet 2

1. F		**11.** S	
2. S		**12.** F	
3. F		**13.** S	
4. F		**14.** F	
5. F		**15.** S	
6. F		**16.** F	
7. F		**17.** F	
8. S		**18.** F	
9. F		**19.** F	
10. F		**20.** F	

p. 3 | **Exercise 2**
PRACTICE A, Worksheet 3

(Answers will vary. Sample answers follow.)

1. S

2. S

3. F **The participants** chose the events.

4. F When my little brother won the watermelon-seed-spitting contest, **we were all surprised.**

5. S

6. F After eating nine slices, **he couldn't eat any more watermelon.**

7. S

8. S

9. F **We all cheered** when she was awarded her prize.

10. F **My big brother w**as a volunteer at the dunking booth.

11. F **He got mad** because I dunked him four times.

12. F When my mom said I couldn't ride on the Screamer, **I went on a different ride.**

13. F While I was on the Whirling Hurricane, **all the change fell out of my pockets.**

14. F Rocky Road and the Detours **performed** at the festival.

15. F **I made sure I got a front-row seat** because they are my favorite band.

p. 4 | **Exercise 2**
PRACTICE B, Worksheet 4

(Answers will vary. Sample answers follow.)

1. S

2. F **It was a** perfect day for a kayak trip down the North Fork River.

3. F The fall air **was** crisp and cool.

4. F **The leaves were f**alling from the trees along the banks.

5. F **We had brought** a lot of equipment, such as life jackets, fishing rods, and picnic supplies.

6. F When we waded into the river to launch our kayaks, **the water felt cold.**

7. F Rainbow trout **were** eating bugs off the surface of the water.

8. S

9. F **We t**ook pictures of all the fish we caught before we let them go.

10. F **We also took pictures of b**irds, squirrels, and even a snake.

11. F Because we were getting hungry, **we stopped and had a picnic.**

12. F The sandwiches and salads **tasted wonderful.**

13. F While getting back into my kayak, **I fell in the river.**

14. *S*

15. *F* By the time we reached the end of our trip, **it was already dark.**

p. 5 | **Exercise 3**
PRACTICE A, Worksheet 5

(Answers will vary. Sample answers follow.)

1. Riding a motorcycle can be a lot of fun, **but** it can also be very dangerous.

2. Motorcycles must share the road with cars and trucks. **These** vehicles outweigh a motorcycle by several tons.

3. *C*

4. Rain can make the surface of the road very slippery. **Loose** gravel can cause a motorcyclist to lose control.

5. It's a good idea to take a course in motorcycle safety. **Courses** are offered by many police departments and motorcycle riders' associations.

6. You'll learn the basics of operating a motorcycle, **and** you'll learn how to react in emergency situations.

7. *C*

8. Many states require riders to protect their eyes. **This** protection keeps insects, stones, and dust out of the eyes.

9. You can wear motorcycle goggles, **or** you can wear sunglasses.

10. The Motorcycle Safety Foundation recommends a full-face helmet. **They** say it is the most important piece of safety equipment.

p. 6 | **Exercise 3**
PRACTICE B, Worksheet 6

(Answers will vary. Sample answers follow.)

1. A cave can be just large enough for one person, **or** it can be as huge as an enormous room.

2. The largest known cave has 550 kilometers of passages, **but** some think it has even more unexplored areas.

3. *C*

4. Water remains in some caves. **It** forms deep underground lakes.

5. One type of cave is formed when underground lava cools first on the outside. **The** molten lava inside then exits, leaving a hollow place.

6. Crashing surf makes "sea caves." **The** water breaks down rock along the shore.

7. A sinkhole is a cave with its entrance in the "roof." **Have** you ever stumbled upon a sinkhole?

8. *C*

9. Stalactites hang from the ceiling of a cave, **and** stalagmites rise from its floor.

10. These cave formations look like icicles and pillars individually, **but** they form a column from floor to ceiling when they connect.

p. 7 | **Review A**
PRACTICE A, Worksheet 7

(Run-on sentences are underlined twice; fragments are underlined once.)

The human brain is made up of three main parts the three parts work together to carry out complicated tasks. The cerebrum is where information from your senses is processed. When your eyes see a skunk in the road. Your cerebrum tells your arms to move the steering wheel to avoid it. The cerebellum controls balance and coordination, this is the part of the brain that helps you hold a soft drink and change the radio station at the same time. When you almost have a head-on collision from trying to do too many things at once. The brain stem brings your heart rate back to normal.

Answer Key *(continued)*

Revised paragraph (Answers will vary. Sample answer follows.)

The human brain is made up of three main parts. **T**he three parts work together to carry out complicated tasks. The cerebrum is where information from your senses is processed. When your eyes see a skunk in the road, **y**our cerebrum tells your arms to move the steering wheel to avoid it. The cerebellum controls balance and coordination. **T**his is the part of the brain that helps you hold a soft drink and change the radio station at the same time. When you almost have a head-on collision from trying to do too many things at once, **t**he brain stem brings your heart rate back to normal.

p. 8 | Review A
PRACTICE B, Worksheet 8

(Run-on sentences are underlined twice; fragments are underlined once.)

The ancient Egyptians preserved the bodies of the dead with a special process of embalming the entire process took about seventy days. One of the first steps was removing the internal organs. Most of the organs taken out and placed in jars. A kind of rock salt was then used to dry the body. Once the body had dried completely. The Egyptians filled it with material to preserve its shape. Different materials were used. They packed the body with linen pads they filled it with sawdust. Next, the body was wrapped in many layers of linen bandages. When the wrapping was completed. The mummy was placed in a coffin. The ancient Egyptians' process very effective. Scientists sometimes unwrap mummies to study them. The bodies have deteriorated, you can still tell what the person looked like when he or she was alive.

Revised paragraph (Answers will vary. Sample answer follows.)

The ancient Egyptians preserved the bodies of the dead with a special process of embalming. **T**he entire process took about seventy days. One of the first steps was removing the internal organs. Most of the organs **were** taken out and placed in jars. A kind of rock salt was then used to dry the body. Once the body had dried completely, **t**he Egyptians filled it with material to preserve its shape. Different materials were used. They packed the body with linen pads, **o**r they filled it with sawdust. Next, the body was wrapped in many layers of linen bandages. When the wrapping was completed, **t**he mummy was placed in a coffin. The ancient Egyptians' process **was** very effective. Scientists sometimes unwrap mummies to study them. The bodies have deteriorated, **but** you can still tell what the person looked like when he or she was alive.

p. 9 | Exercise 4
PRACTICE A, Worksheet 9

(Answers will vary. Sample answers follow.)

1. A horse is born ready to stand on its own **four** legs.
2. However, a kangaroo is born **partially** developed.
3. A newborn kangaroo must climb into its mother's **warm** pouch.
4. The baby kangaroo grows **slowly** in the pouch.
5. The kangaroo will have large, **powerful** hind legs as an adult.
6. Kangaroos use their **strong** hind legs to hop at speeds up to thirty miles per hour.
7. A kangaroo uses its **long** tail for support and balance.
8. Kangaroos' **useful** ears can twist forward and backward.

9. Kangaroos are preyed upon by **Australian** dogs called dingoes.

10. **Strict** laws protect kangaroos from human hunters.

p. 10 | Exercise 4
PRACTICE B, Worksheet 10

(Answers will vary. Sample answers follow.)

1. Sleep is an **important** state shared by human beings and animals.

2. Scientists study people's **sleeping** habits.

3. A **highly** sensitive machine can show how the brain functions during sleep.

4. Waking people's brains give off about ten **small** electrical waves per second.

5. **Varying b**rain waves continue during sleep.

6. People need both slow-moving and fast-moving brain waves for **restful** sleep.

7. People have **rapid** eye movements when they experience fast-moving brain waves.

8. **Vivid d**reams occur during REM (rapid eye movement) sleep.

9. People sometimes question what their **puzzling** dreams mean.

10. People who are prevented from entering deep sleep **eventually** become irritable.

p. 11 | Exercise 5
PRACTICE A, Worksheet 11

(Answers will vary. Sample answers follow.)

1. Today, travelers can cross the United States **by airplane** in a matter of hours.

2. The eight-thousand-mile journey of Meriwether Lewis and William Clark, **the leaders of the Lewis and Clark expedition,** was no vacation.

3. **Hoping to establish a route to the Pacific coast,** President Thomas Jefferson sent a team of explorers westward.

4. In 1804, the group led by Lewis and Clark set out from St. Louis on its journey **to explore the northwestern region.**

5. The explorers had problems from the very beginning of the journey, **having to paddle their heavy boats upstream against the swift current of the Missouri River.**

6. The explorers tried to establish good relations with the American Indians they met **by giving them presents.**

7. Many people the explorers met were friendly, **eager to offer food and advice.**

8. Sacagawea, **a Shoshone woman,** joined the expedition team as an interpreter.

9. **After crossing the Bitterroot Mountains,** the team began a very difficult part of its journey.

10. When they reached the Pacific Ocean, they built a fort where they spent the winter, **gathering strength for their long trip home.**

p. 12 | Exercise 5
PRACTICE B, Worksheet 12

(Answers will vary. Sample answers follow.)

1. **To find food or better living conditions, m**any animals migrate from the place where they were born.

2. Some animals, **like the Pacific salmon,** make one great journey in their lifetime.

3. Salmon are born in freshwater streams but live most of their adult lives in the ocean, **returning upstream to spawn.**

4. After spawning, the Pacific salmon dies, **having completed its life cycle.**

5. Other animals migrate annually, **making a round-trip journey.**

6. **Sensing the change of seasons, s**ome birds go south for the winter.

7. Scientists believe that a bird's "inner calendar," **present at birth,** tells it when to return home in the spring.

8. The arctic tern is one of the record holders for long-distance migrations, **traveling up to 22,000 miles in a year.**

9. Adult humpback whales spend most of their time **in the icy water of the polar regions** where their food supply is most abundant.

10. When a female whale is ready to give birth, she and her mate migrate to warmer tropical waters **for the sake of the newborn calf.**

p. 13 | Exercise 6
PRACTICE A, Worksheet 13

(Answers will vary. Sample answers follow.)

1. Toads and frogs belong to a group of animals called amphibians.

2. Amphibians can survive in the water and live on land.

3. Female toads and frogs can lay thousands of eggs at a time.

4. Tadpoles hatch from the eggs and remain in the water as they mature into adult frogs.

5. Toads do not like direct sunlight and are most active during rainy days or at night.

6. People do not get warts from toads but may get sick from touching a toad's back.

7. Toads burrow or hibernate to escape extreme weather.

8. Frogs and toads are beneficial to humans because they eat insect pests.

9. The cane toad is one of the largest toads and can grow up to nine inches in length.

10. The Goliath frog of West Africa is the largest frog and weighs about seven pounds.

p. 14 | Exercise 6
PRACTICE B, Worksheet 14

(Answers will vary. Sample answers follow.)

1. Alligators and crocodiles are reptiles.

2. Both animals' eyes sit high on their heads and let them see above water.

3. Crocodiles use their short, strong legs for walking on land and swim by moving their tails from side to side.

4. A crocodile looks much like an alligator but weighs only about two-thirds as much.

5. Crocodiles eat small animals such as fish and birds and occasionally attack large animals and people.

6. Alligators and crocodiles have long snouts and sharp teeth.

7. An alligator's snout is long but broader and more rounded than a crocodile's snout.

8. Crocodiles hide their eggs in nests of brush or leaves or bury their eggs in the sand.

9. Crocodiles and alligators were once widely hunted for their hides.

10. Alligators were once classified as an endangered species but have been reclassified because their numbers are increasing.

p. 15 | Exercise 7
PRACTICE A, Worksheet 15

(Answers will vary. Sample answers follow.)

1. This desert has one of the world's harshest climates, and large portions of it are completely uninhabited.

2. The word *Sahara* comes from the Arabic word for desert, but different parts of this desert have other names.

3. The Sahara contains valuable minerals such as copper, iron, tin, and gold, but many of these have not yet been mined.

4. The Saharan climate is hot and dry, but the air turns cool at night.

5. Much of the desert consists of vast seas of sand called *ergs*, and the shifting sand in these ergs can form dunes as high as 600 feet.

6. The landscape of the Sahara does not change for mile after mile, and this is probably why it is nicknamed "ocean of the sands."

7. People believe that a continuous sandy landscape is typical of the Sahara, but this terrain accounts for only one eighth of the desert's area.

8. The Painted Desert in Arizona differs in character from the Sahara, and its name indicates its more colorful terrain.

Answer Key (continued)

9. Its brightly colored rocks impressed a U.S. government explorer, and he chose the name "painted" to describe the place.

10. Navajo and Hopi reservations are part of the Painted Desert, and the Navajo use the colorful sands to make ceremonial paintings.

p. 16 | Exercise 7
PRACTICE B, Worksheet 16

(Answers will vary. Sample answers follow.)

1. Earthquakes damaged the ancient city in A.D. 62, but it was a volcanic eruption that ultimately destroyed Pompeii.

2. Pompeii was not famous in its time, but it is better known today because its ruins are so well preserved.

3. Mount Vesuvius erupted violently in the summer of A.D. 79, and Pompeii was engulfed in hot ashes and poisonous gases.

4. When the ashes fell on Pompeii, much of the city was buried, and only columns and rooftops were left visible.

5. Survivors recovered some valuables that they had left behind in the city, but later eruptions buried any remaining items.

6. Almost 1,400 years later, people knew of the buried city, but no one paid much attention to it.

7. In 1748, a man was digging in a vineyard, and his shovel hit a buried wall.

8. Italian historians were excited by the discovery, and archaeologists soon began to excavate, hoping to find important artifacts.

9. Archaeologists decided to leave many objects where they were found, and they began restoring the site to its original condition.

10. After ongoing excavation, about three fourths of Pompeii is visible, and visitors can see how the Pompeians lived.

p. 17 | Exercise 8
PRACTICE A, Worksheet 17

(Answers will vary. Sample answers follow.)

1. A banjo is a stringed musical instrument that combines a guitar neck with a body like a tambourine.

2. The banjo was developed in Africa before it was brought to America.

3. The body of the banjo is covered with animal skin or plastic that is stretched over a round frame.

4. This body gives the banjo its characteristic sound when its strings are plucked.

5. A five-string banjo's shortest string, which is known as the "thumb string," is fastened to a screw in the neck.

6. My sister decided to play the banjo after she listened to a famous banjo picker.

7. She has become an enthusiastic banjo student, who practices night and day.

8. Fingerpicking is a style of banjo playing that is said to "sparkle."

9. My sister is good at frailing, which is a way of strumming the banjo instead of picking it.

10. People cannot help but dance when banjo players start strumming and picking.

p. 18 | Exercise 8
PRACTICE B, Worksheet 18

(Answers will vary. Sample answers follow.)

1. John Cabot, an Italian who explored for England, discovered Newfoundland in 1497.

2. He spread the word about the area, where fish were plentiful.

3. Many fishing boats came from different countries after people heard the news.

4. Fishing crews competed for the area, which they knew could supply a lot of food.

5. Communities of fishing camps existed for many years before the area finally became a colony in 1824.

6. Its people showed their strong independence when they refused to become Canadians until 1949.

7. Part of Newfoundland is an island that is separated from the mainland by the Strait of Belle Isle.

8. The rest of Newfoundland is made up of the Labrador coast, which is part of the Canadian mainland.

9. Newfoundland's largest city is St. John's, which is also the capital of the province.

10. The area has a wild, rugged seacoast that stretches for 10,000 miles.

p. 19 | Review B
PRACTICE A, Worksheet 19

(Answers will vary. Sample answer follows.)

   Atlantic puffins are seabirds that nest along northern seacoasts. They spend most of their adult lives far out at sea, coming to land only to nest. After the parents dig a hole in the ground three to six feet deep, the female usually lays one white egg, and both adults incubate it for more than a month. When the chick hatches, it stays warm—or "broods"—under its parents' wings for a few days. Puffins can be identified by their bright, multicolored beaks. "Sea parrot," "clown of the sea," and "bottlenose" are nicknames for these colorful birds. They are clumsy fliers but graceful and efficient swimmers, propelling themselves with their wings and using their feet to steer. Puffins are comical in appearance, but they are talented fishers.

p. 20 | Review B
PRACTICE B, Worksheet 20

(Answers will vary. Sample answer follows.)

   Gray meerkats, a type of mongoose, live in the Kalahari Desert in southern Africa. They travel in groups and hunt for insects during the day. Because meerkats are small, they are often hunted by birds of prey. Meerkats cannot dig for insects and watch for predators at the same time. For this reason, some meerkats hunt while others stand guard. The guards take their job very seriously, staying on constant lookout for danger. Later, other meerkats stand watch, so the guards get a chance to eat. Because meerkats are more vulnerable alone, cooperation is necessary for survival.

p. 21 | Exercise 9
PRACTICE A, Worksheet 21

(Answers will vary. Sample answers follow.)

1. C

2. Lightning can also be deadly, killing about 100 Americans every year.

3. Benjamin Franklin used a kite to help prove that lightning was made of electricity, but his experiment was very dangerous. Franklin was lucky that he was not killed.

4. The safest place to be during an electrical storm is inside a building. You can also take shelter inside a car, but be careful not to touch any of the metal parts.

5. Lightning can travel through telephone lines, striking people through the phone. Because of this, you should not use a telephone during a thunderstorm.

6. Because lightning often strikes water, it is dangerous to be in a pool during a thunderstorm. That is why lifeguards clear the pool when they see lightning.

7. C

8. Standing under a tall tree during a thunderstorm is not a good idea. If lightning strikes the tree, it can jump from the tree to nearby objects.

p. 22 | Exercise 9
PRACTICE B, Worksheet 22

(Answers will vary. Sample answers follow.)

1. Our hair does much more than keep our ears warm. It can have a big effect on how we feel about ourselves and can be used to express our individuality.

2. When we think our hair looks good, we feel more confident and able to face the world.

Answer Key (continued)

3. All it takes is one bad haircut to make a person want to flee from society and hide under a bed until his or her hair grows out. This can take a long time, since hair grows only about half an inch a month.

4. Hair can be changed with a snip of the scissors or by curling, straightening, or dyeing.

5. Because we can do so many different things with our hair, our hairstyles become a mode of self-expression. People often make statements about who they are by how they style their hair.

6. C

7. To do the opposite of what "everyone" is doing, some people wear unique hairstyles that set them apart from the crowd.

8. Because styles are as unique and individualized as the people wearing them, different styles make the world more interesting.

p. 23 | Exercise 10
PRACTICE A, Worksheet 23

(Answers will vary. Sample answers follow.)

1. Curious, the baby will use all five senses to explore the new toy.

2. Our ancestors probably explored the world in much the same way, using their senses to learn about their environment.

3. However, the moon was too far away for people to explore with any sense except sight.

4. Because the moon changed, it was a natural subject for stories.

5. C

6. Early scientists offered a variety of explanations about life on the moon, and one believed the craters were built by moon creatures.

7. In 1609, Galileo, an Italian astronomer, became the first person to study the moon with a telescope.

8. Some writers imagined traveling to the moon using antigravity devices or huge cannons to propel them.

9. The first moon landing, in 1969, provided scientists with new information about the moon.

10. The astronauts brought back samples of moon rocks, proving beyond a doubt that the moon is NOT made of cheese.

p. 24 | Exercise 10
PRACTICE B, Worksheet 24

(Answers will vary. Sample answers follow.)

1. These people, eager to learn about aquatic life firsthand, would climb right into the aquarium if they could.

2. This desire to explore the world of fish and aquatic plants gave birth to the sport of scuba diving.

3. Scuba diving, a relatively new sport, is becoming increasingly popular.

4. Throughout history, people have been diving in search of fish, shells, and treasure.

5. Until scuba gear was invented, divers could stay underwater for only as long as they could hold their breath.

6. Some could stay under as long as three minutes, but this was dangerous because divers can pass out underwater.

7. C

8. Public swimming pools and colleges sometimes offer courses to teach people to scuba dive.

9. In a scuba-diving course, you will learn that you should never scuba dive by yourself.

10. You will also learn how to avoid dangerous sea creatures.

p. 25 | **Exercise 11**
PRACTICE A, Worksheet 25

(Answers will vary. Sample answer follows.)

To become a fly fisher, you must master certain skills and learn a lot about fish. You must learn how to assemble your fly rod and how to cast. You must cast the fly so that it drops onto the water like a snowflake and keep the line from slapping the water. It might not sound difficult, but novice fly fishers often spend hours untangling fishing line. You also need to learn where to find fish and what they like to eat. It can all seem like a lot of hard work just to catch a fish. However, catching that first beautiful trout on a fly rod makes it all worthwhile. You will think you found the gold at the end of the rainbow!

p. 26 | **Exercise 11**
PRACTICE B, Worksheet 26

(Answers will vary. Sample answer follows.)

Earth seems to be "solid as a rock," but its outer shell is actually made of slow-moving, rocky plates. As they slide past each other, the plates sometimes collide, creating great pressure on the outer edges of the plates. This pressure increases until the rocks break under the strain, creating an earthquake. Most earthquakes occur in the "Ring of Fire," the land that rings the Pacific Ocean. The largest earthquakes in the United States occurred in New Madrid, Missouri, in the early 1800s. The largest of these New Madrid earthquakes was felt from Canada to the Gulf of Mexico and changed the course of the Mississippi River.

p. 27 | **Review C**
PRACTICE A, Worksheet 27

(Answers will vary. Sample answer follows.)

Who can forget the thrill of learning to ride a bicycle? However, the thrill wears off as bicycles become our main transportation. Then, once we get our driver's licenses, we don't even use our bicycles. They are stored away in the garage, serving no purpose and gathering dust. Now, though, with the development of the mountain bike, people are rediscovering the pleasure of biking that they first experienced as children. With its sturdy frame and knobby tires, the mountain bike is luring adults out to play. It has brought bicyclists out in force to embrace and explore the land beyond the pavement. The mountain-bike trails that wind through the nation's parks help adults satisfy the need to explore, which never really goes away.

p. 28 | **Review C**
PRACTICE B, Worksheet 28

(Answers will vary. Sample answer follows.)

A dollar bill is just a piece of paper with no value in and of itself. Dollar bills, as well as coins, checks, and credit cards, have value because we all agree that they do. Before money was invented, people had to trade what they had for what they wanted, a system much less convenient than paying with money. This was known as the barter system. People used to trade animal hides, cloth, animals, or other goods and services to get what they wanted. However, the system did not always work. What if you went to the market to trade your goat for some chickens, and the person who had chickens to trade already had enough goats? You would have to go home without a chicken. This problem is solved when there is an agreed-upon monetary system. People accept money because they know they can use it to buy many different things. It's hard to imagine a world without some kind of monetary system. If money had never been invented, would people have to take a couple of goats to the shopping mall instead of credit cards?

Answer Key *(continued)*

Chapter 9

Learning About Paragraphs

p. 29 | **Exercise 1**
   Worksheet 29

1. **Topic sentence:** Many people know an orca when they see one.

2. **Topic sentence:** There are some common misconceptions about orcas.

3. **Main idea:** *(Answers will vary. Sample answer follows.)* Orcas are effective hunters.

4. **Topic sentence:** Orcas are called killers not because of their behavior toward humans, but because of the way they treat other ocean creatures.

p. 30 | **Exercise 2**
   Worksheet 30

(Answers will vary. Sample answers follow.)

1. **Topic sentence:** A simple change in the shape of the ice ax gave birth to the new sport of ice climbing.

2. **Topic sentence:** Climbers can now go places that were off-limits before.

3. **Topic sentence:** Mountaineers find ice climbing exciting for several reasons.

4. **Topic sentence:** A person has to be in excellent shape to ice climb.

5. **Topic sentence:** Ice climbing is not for casual climbers.

p. 31 | **Exercise 3**
   Worksheet 31

(Answers will vary, but should develop the main idea presented.)

p. 32 | **Exercise 4**
   Worksheet 32

(Answers will vary, but should sum up the information in the paragraph. Sample answers follow.)

1. Penguins are more widespread than many people think.

2. Telling one species from another requires careful observation.

3. Even though feathers do not help a penguin fly, they are still very important for its survival.

4. In the water, penguins are as graceful as dolphins.

5. Penguins get around on land quite well, despite how they look.

p. 33 | **Exercise 5**
   Worksheet 33

1. Venus is the second planet from the sun.

2. Venus is named for the goddess of love.

3. The planet was called Phosphorus.

4. Radar images suggest that Venus may have sand dunes.

5. Venus rotates once every 243 Earth days.

p. 34 | **Exercise 6**
   Worksheet 34

(Answers will vary, but all details should be organized in chronological order.)

p. 35 | **Exercise 7**
   Worksheet 35

(Answers will vary, but all details should be organized in spatial order.)

p. 36 | **Exercise 8**
   Worksheet 36

(Answers will vary, but all details should be organized in logical order.)

p. 37 | Exercise 9
Worksheet 37

(Transitional words and phrases are underlined.)

1. "It's going to storm," warned Grandmother, pointing to birds way up in the afternoon sky. Only a few clouds were in sight, but I knew she was right. <u>When</u> a thunderstorm is forming, warm, moist air flows upward. <u>Consequently</u>, flying insects are drawn up, too. <u>Because</u> the insects are higher, birds must fly higher than usual to catch and eat them. <u>As a result</u>, the birds provide a sign that the atmosphere is right for developing thunderstorms. The swallows we saw were flying so high that we could barely see them. Grandmother and I <u>therefore</u> checked the TV weather forecast, and just as Grandmother thought, rain was expected.

2. Do you think crayons are just for little kids? Think again. Just about everyone, from preschoolers to professional artists, loves crayons. Crayons are so popular, <u>in fact</u>, that some clubs work to preserve their history. In 1991, <u>for example</u>, these clubs protested when several old crayon colors were replaced with new, updated colors. <u>In addition to</u> liking the colors themselves, people like the expressive names of some crayons, such as *plum jam* for purple. People are <u>also</u> crazy about the scent of crayons. <u>For example</u>, their waxy smell is one of the top twenty scents recognized by adults. Clearly, crayons are not just for kids!

3. Add together a cloudless night, a group of campers, and several telescopes, and what do you have? A star party, of course. Star parties take place at national parks, state campgrounds, and observatories—anywhere far from light sources such as cities.

The night sky has to be very dark for the stars to show up well. <u>Before</u> the party begins, a park ranger or astronomer explains which constellations or planets are visible at that time of year. <u>When</u> darkness finally arrives, the Milky Way splashes its 200 billion stars across the sky, and it's time for the party to begin. Campers step up to telescopes and focus. <u>Suddenly</u>, Saturn's rings seem huge and bright. The moon's craters look truly deep. <u>When</u> the stars begin to fade around dawn, campers stumble into tents to sleep all day.

p. 38 | Exercise 10
Worksheet 38

(Answers will vary. Sample answers follow.)

1. Setting up a successful trip to the mall can be harder than it seems. First, you have to decide whether to go alone or with friends. If you go alone, you will probably get things done faster, but if you take a friend, you will probably have more fun. Next, there is the matter of getting there. For me, taking the bus is the best solution so I don't have to depend on someone else's schedule. Most important, you have to have a good game plan about how to spend your time there. If you're going to shop, shop. If you're going to hang out, hang out. The important thing is to decide in advance.

2. It is really very easy to tell good movies from bad ones. Good movies have an interesting story, plenty of complicating details, and maybe a little mystery. They usually have talented actors who make you believe the plot. They are also fun to watch. In a really good movie, you don't want to look away from the screen for even a couple of seconds. Bad movies might have one or two good points, such as an interesting character or a good idea, but bad movies usually leave you feeling bored or confused. Sometimes they drag on and on, and sometimes the plots are so confusing

you get lost. When a bad movie is over, you find yourself saying, "Boy, that was stupid."

3. Families should prepare themselves for the possibility of extreme weather. Sometimes when the weather gets really bad, such as during tornadoes or hurricanes, people have to do without electricity and water. Sometimes bad weather causes flooding, which can make it impossible to leave your home. When you can't leave your home, getting food can be a problem. The food in your refrigerator can spoil if the electricity is out. It's a good idea to have canned food and nonperishable food on hand just to be safe. If people were prepared by having some flashlights, bottled water, and canned food on hand, then extreme weather would not seem like such a problem.

**p. 39 | Exercise 11
Worksheet 39**

1. Narrative—the writer is telling the story of how the kitten is taking over the family.

2. Persuasive—the writer is trying to convince the audience that cats do not make good pets.

3. Expository—the writer is listing facts about the history of domesticated cats.

**p. 40 | Exercise 12
Worksheet 40**

Have you ever been to a kite-flying contest? If you have, then you know that there are lots of unique and unusual kites being flown today. Kites come in all shapes and sizes and can be made with many different kinds of materials. Most people are familiar with the fairly simple diamond-shaped kites made of wooden sticks and paper. Kites, however, may be made of cloth or plastic and may be shaped like rectangles, triangles, squares, or even hexagons.

Kites get their name from a bird called a "kite." This hawklike bird glides on air currents while searching for prey. When it sees a mouse or an insect, it suddenly swerves, dips, or soars upward, chasing its prey. In a similar manner, a kite flown by people hovers in the sky and, with the jerk of a string, dives with a sudden whoosh or dances wildly across the sky.

People in Asia have been flying kites as far back as recorded history. In some countries, such as China, Japan, Korea, and Malaysia, kite flying is a national pastime. Kites have symbolic significance in some of these countries and are flown on ceremonial occasions.

An American famous for kite flying is Ben Franklin. According to legend, he hung a metal key on his kite line and flew the kite in a thunderstorm. As Franklin reportedly expected, the key attracted electricity from the air, providing evidence that lightning is electrical in nature.

Because most people do not wish to be struck by lightning, modern kite flyers should think of Franklin's experience as a lesson about kite-flying conditions to avoid. Bad weather certainly can be dangerous to kite flyers, but it is not the only threat. Electrical wires can also be very hazardous. The best way to fly a kite is on a clear day, out in the open. The wind should be strong enough to keep the kite in the air, but not so strong that it will tear the kite to pieces. Ideally the wind should be between eight and twenty miles an hour. Never fly a kite in damp weather or near power lines.

Explanation for Paragraph Breaks:

The first paragraph discusses the materials used to make kites. The second paragraph discusses the origin of the word *kite*. The third paragraph discusses the historical significance of kites in Asian countries. In the fourth paragraph, the writer discusses an American historical kite-flying event. The final paragraph discusses conditions for kite flying.